Misconception and Orthodoxy

(Vol- 1)

ভ্রান্ত বিশ্বাস ও গোঁড়ামি (১. খণ্ড)

Ni_ _ondal

ISBN 978-93-5559-122-7
© NK Mondal 2021
Published in India 2021 by Pencil

A brand of

One Point Six Technologies Pvt. Ltd.
123, Building J2, Shram Seva Premises,
Wadala Truck Terminal, Wadala (E)
Mumbai 400037, Maharashtra, INDIA
E connect@thepencilapp.com
W www.thepencilapp.com

Author biography

N.K.Mondal (Hindi: एन.के.मंडल)(Bengali: এন.কে.মণ্ডল) is an indian bengali poet,writer, social adviser, script writer, columnist, and novelist from the state of West bengal, India.He is also a writer.He was awarded with the title of Sahitya Ratna.

Personal Life :

Mondal was born on 5 may 1996 from Murshidabad district in India.His parents Saiful Islam and Menuka Bibi used to lovingly call him Salim.He passed higher secondary examination from Rukanpur High School, Murshidabad.He earned degree in bachelor of arts from Hazi A.K.Khan College, University of Kalyni

Poetry:

Pratibad

Amar desh

Amar dida

Sandha

Bikel bela

Dinguli

Paltacche

Swamaj

Onek boro

Sajur Chayer dokan

Bose achi

Boudir gosol

Tin mather more

Bharat Pakistan

Stories:

Premer Atha

Prem

Premer Chabial

Premer Chhyaka

Adbhuture Kanda

Adhkhana Banger Baccha

Swapner Thikana

Adarshya Prem

Bartaman Manab Charitra

Ami N.K.Mondal

Adhapotan

Pratyabartan

Prachin Bari

Somoyer Byastota

Books:

Ananda Path

Akash Chhoya Mon

Bhalobashar Posh Chhoya

Rohosyamoi Prachin Bari[6]

Thamthampur

Education:

Hazi A.K.Khan College

Rukanpur High School

Char Muktarpur High Madrasa

Pratappur Shishu Shikhsa Kendra

Berhampore Para Medical College

CONTENTS

Volume - 1

The lexical meaning of the word misconception is misconception That is, there must be misconceptions in human life, that is normal and subject to real reasoning Every human being had a misconception, has and will have 7 No matter how great a human being is, there were mistakes in life And some of those misconceptions will be discussed with proper reasoning Basically, I will try to expose the misconceptions about God and religion

| | Chapter One | |

1. Will God give anything else to man?

People usually say, "If you ask God, you can get everything." However, no proof has been found so far as to how true this statement is Evidence of what has been found is in the story, in the dream, in the belief and in the devotion In general, most superstitious superstitions put people in danger, which is proven Various believers have said, "If you ask God, you can get everything." For believers, God or Almighty can be obtained by asking Him. He does not disappoint anyone, but I do not believe that. Millions of people around the world worship God and ask for more, but they do not get it without doing it. He has to work hard to get that thing God will give directly, as the magicians do But God doesn't really do that to mankind, He has to take action No matter how big he is and no matter how cowardly God is If God does not give directly, then you have to take action, then why ask God Many, especially religious teachers, say that "the prayers of such and such a person have been accepted by God, given to him by those who have given him" are just stories and history. Has anyone received anything from God today? There is no evidence Even religion teachers did not get it But what will the common man get? Usually God will not give anything to the human race That is the real thing Many may get angry at my writing, But don't leave a comment without reading it completely. It is 99% true that there is no worldly thing with God Because he sent people to the earth to survive He has sent hands, feet, eyes, ears, nose and important intellect for human action Each limb has a specific function পরতৃযা These were originally given to man by God. 6 for the restoration of human action, hunger, etc. At the same time, he has already given all the human needs for the worldly needs of the people There is nothing left, but we always ask God through prayer God can only give something spiritual or human beings can ask for something spiritual, which is possible. If the various believers think that they can get what they want from God, then what is the need of human money for the work of God, that is, for building a temple? Since it is a temple or house of God, That is why at least God can create or ask Him collectively, because one cannot listen to the other. Or teachers of religion may ask the Creator for a place of worship Why do people have to beg for a place of worship? All the necessities of human life were given by God immediately after the creation of the world, for which man needs nothing else. All I have to ask is, God, to guide me to the straight path. Protect me from evil deeds like gossip, violence, loss and so on It is possible to ask God for work like that, which is possible And they have to take care of themselves But they should not be left to God alone, they should be practiced Practice root 6 If someone says I won't pass the test, I will pass, But isn't that a fool's errand? That is, a person prayed to God that he would not pass the test, but would pass the test and be the first. Will God make him pass the test at all? No, he will not pass, because he did not pass the test No one can ever pass the exam without it That is, not everything is available to God That is, all the work of the world cannot be obtained by asking God, He must do the work This is real or true Because he has given everything for man, because the world is a test for man He handed over all the notebooks, pens, question papers etc. before reaching the examination hall. That is, if you do action, you will be able to eat This is the eternal truth Because he did not give the test No one can ever pass the exam without it That is, not everything is available to God That is, all the work of the world cannot be obtained by asking God, He must do the work This is real or true Because he has given everything for man, because the world is a test for man He handed over all the notebooks, pens, question papers etc. before reaching the examination hall. That is, if you do action, you will be able to eat This is the eternal truth Because he did not give the test No one can ever pass the exam without it That is, not everything is available to God That is, all the work of the world cannot be obtained by asking God, He must do the work This is real or true Because he has given everything for man, because the world is a test for man He handed over all the notebooks, pens, question papers etc. before reaching the examination hall. That is, if you do action, you will be able to eat This is the eternal truth

God does not give anything worldly to anyone, human beings always have to get work

2. God manages the human race as a power

God is basically omnipotent He is the sole owner of all things But he does not use the most powerful form for the human race He has given everything on earth except the specified lifespan for the needs of the human race God is the only tester in the world He does not make anyone rich or poor He does not harm anyone, he does not oppress anyone, if he did these things then God would not be great and great. Because if one is made rich and the other is made poor, that is why the creation of the same God is different, then what is the right thing God has done? Many people say that God has made me rich, then what is the fault of others? There is no fault of God here, everything that has happened has been done by deeds God wants the best for everyone God does not use His all-powerful form, because He is a tester The sole purpose of sending mankind to earth is to worship God, And in order to achieve this goal, all the work of the world becomes urgent for human beings Many ask me if I do not see God, my family does not go, and the family of the village headman is growing day by day, but I do not get anything by worshiping God. That is to say, God makes one happy and the other miserable, which is basically a misconception of man. And if God makes one happy and the other miserable, then what is the true judgment of God? To him all people are equal, and if that is not the case then why did he make people the same in the world Two hands, two feet, two eyes are all equal, then why did God not spare anyone from that, but why did He separate them from the worldly work of the world. Many may say that many are handicapped Yes, that's right If one out of ten crows is lame, not all crows can be called lame. My family does not survive, and the family of the village headman is growing day by day, but I do not get anything by worshiping God. That is to say, God makes one happy and the other miserable, which is basically a misconception of man. And if God makes one happy and the other miserable, then what is the true judgment of God? To him all people are equal, and if that is not the case then why did he make people the same in the world Two hands, two feet, two eyes are all equal, then why did God not spare anyone from that, but why did He separate them from the worldly work of the world. Many may say that many are handicapped Yes, that's right If one out of ten crows is lame, not all crows can be called lame. My family does not survive, and the family of the village headman is growing day by day, but I do not get anything by worshiping God. That is to say, God makes one happy and the other miserable, which is basically a misconception of man. And if God makes one happy and the other miserable, then what is the true judgment of God? To him all people are equal, and if that is not the case then why did he make people the same in the world Two hands, two feet, two eyes are all equal, then why did God not spare anyone from that, but why did He separate them from the worldly work of the world. Many may say that many are handicapped Yes, that's right If one out of ten crows is lame, not all crows can be called lame. If Khee, then what is the correct judgment of God To him all people are equal, and if that is not the case then why did he make people the same in the world Two hands, two feet, two eyes are all equal, then why did God not spare anyone from that, but why did He separate them from the worldly work of the world. Many may say that many are handicapped Yes, that's right If one out of ten crows is lame, not all crows can be called lame. If Khee, then what is the correct judgment of God To him all people are equal, and if that is not the case then why did he make people the same in the world Two hands, two feet, two eyes are all equal, then why did God not spare anyone from that, but why did He separate them from the worldly work of the world. Many may say that many are handicapped Yes, that's right If one out of ten crows is lame, not all crows can be called lame.

3. What God basically does

God is basically the most powerful personality He is the owner of all things He manages all the work with the help of his staff Therefore, he has distributed various departments Someone food, water, weather, etc. 6 Many do not agree, but it is seen in different religious scriptures that it is said about different departments

4. Does God control or manage people?

God does not control or guide any human being He is the most powerful personality He is the Creator and the Judge of creation He does not guide man, because he has given man the brain to manage I If God had guided man, man would not have sinned If God guides man, then why should there be a judgment of good and evil of man, since he rules knowingly, I think I need a statement in this regard.

"God created you in the best possible way and sent you into the world to be perfect. You have been given an excellent brain to judge between good and evil. That will be enough to guide you." Originally, if God guides man, then the good and the bad of man will be the fault of God, why man will be the fault, for him or why heaven and hell.

5. Is God one or the same?

God is basically one or unique He is the Creator He is the most powerful person He is above all Some religious people say that this is God, this is God, but they know that there is only one God.

6. Who and what is God?

God is basically an imaginary belief in man No one has ever seen him Many people say that such and such a person has seen such and such a person, but to me they are just stories, which have no reality. And it may be that he introduced himself as a devotee of the great God Blind believers may believe them, but I don't think true God believers and free thinkers will believe them. But it must be acknowledged that God is one, He is omnipotent, He is the Creator and Owner of all creation. He controls everything but does not, but controls the people, except the human race.

|| Chapter Two ||

Religious

1. What is religion and what is it called?

The lexical meaning of the word religion is to hold That is to say, if we understand this word, it is understood that religion is an action which is very necessary for human life In human life, to accept the good qualities from evil deeds in one's mind and to implement them at the same time Besides, religion refers to the characteristics of living beings and objects There is also a common social group religion

2. What is the form of religion

First of all, there is no literal form of the word religion, but the form of social group religion is the form of belief and fiction.

3. How many types of religion and what

Religion is first of two types Religion and unrighteousness 7 There are probably more than 4,000 traditional religions, some of which are still in use today, and most of which are extinct. The majority of those that exist are Christians, Jews, Islam, Buddhists, Hindus, etc. The first religion of the world was Abrahamic religion or Judaism

4. Does conventional religion apply to human life?

Religion is a necessity of human life, but not unrighteousness But now religion is a political role model With which human life can be punished But even if they practice religion, they practice religion on the basis of society or under social pressure, but in reality, it is understood that no religion survives at present, all are standing in the guise of religion.

5. What is religion and what is righteous?

Religion and religion are not one One is a different Religion refers to the qualities or characteristics 7 Righteous is the multiplier He is a personality Religion is not a personality Many people think that religion is the only religion that is a part of the social group But basically they are ignorant Again, many people think that a person who practices religion is called religious, but this is not so strong Because righteous means possessing, while on the other hand it means principled personality

6. Is religion sent by God?

Even in modern science and the light age, many believe that religion is inspired by God People of almost all religions have accepted this with faith But to this day I do not think that a righteous person has ever found out which religion is really sent by God. And why did God give so many religions in the world? People of all religions believe that their religion is sent by God, but aren't other religions sent by God?

Christianity and Islam 6 Apart from this, no religion is sent by God The link between these religions is the same, but some principles have changed

7. If religion is so good then why there is so much rioting about religion with one religion or another religion

At present there is nothing to say about religion Which contains iniquity 6 Every pious person pursues his own interests in the name of religion In fact, there is a famine of the righteous, so there is a riot between one righteous man and another righteous man But in fact there is no riot of one religion with another If the human race knew the meaning of the word religion, then there should be no riot with anyone The pious think that their religion is the best When they speak insultingly in the name of their religion or religious principles, they roar like lions, agitate, destroy the religious institutions of others, destroy government property, and burn down the houses of the insulters. So are they righteous? How many offenders committed crimes, and how many crimes did they commit? The rioters deserve more punishment than the insulter has done wrong In fact, no religion is to blame, The only fault of the righteous is in the name of righteousness Without knowing anything, they fall into the trap of religious teachers and become rioters That is why a person cannot be guilty of religion or principle The only religious war in the world has been provocative, and the only culprits are uneducated religious teachers and orthodox God-worshipers, but they know that God does not really support them.

8. Does religion support orthodoxy?

Another lexical meaning of the word religion is morality That is, morality is never orthodoxy, so religion does not support orthodoxy but opposition. Orthodoxy is a word that is also anti-religion, but this orthodoxy is born of the righteous. Defeated by orthodox free thinkers That is to say, the source of the originator of orthodoxy is the righteous and the source of death is the free thinker and social reformer. Orthodoxy is usually due to boredom, ignorance, lack of knowledge, lack of knowledge of religious law, etc. It is common for people to be orthodox, but the root cause is illiteracy and religion. Basically, these two are responsible

9. Usually the religious upper class does not even hate the work of eating in the lower class house, for example, Muchi Methar Das, etc. Is that right?

Even in the present progressive age, this issue does not make the human conscience conscious, because even in the age of light, not a single drop of human superstition has been allowed to allow orthodoxy to prevail from the very beginning. Even with so many superstitious thinkers in Bengal, Bengal and its environs have not been free from superstition.

First of all, I would like to say that a high class religious person, that is, a Hindu and a Muslim, does not oppose eating in a lower class house. It is proven in the Indian subcontinent A Muslim or a high Hindu shoemaker does not eat in the house of Methar or a small nation But why Many people say that the Muchi or Hajra community is a small nation and they do not eat much because they keep pigs. Hindus are divided into many small castes, they do not go along with such castes, do not eat, do not mix, do not even sit next to them. Is that right? Is it the work of a true believer or a righteous person? Not the work of the ungodly If a person is a true human being, he will never discriminate against human beings You have to eat in every house, you can't think big or small And whoever has these in his head, then he can never be righteous

10. What is heaven by fighting religion.

First of all, I strongly oppose this issue

It is basically an unjust and extreme crime Religion means war in many ways There are two main reasons for the war of religion The first reason is that others are forced to practice their religion The second reason is slander and riots in religious matters But for whatever reason, religious warfare is a major crime

What is heaven by fighting religion 7 It can be said that no These are basically more frequent Orthodoxy and terrorism 7 No religion can command war But the teachers of religion, with the help of God, put the extremists to war God never likes blood Whoever does that will enjoy the fruits of his deeds in this world and in the next world Religion can never find heaven by fighting The Crusades are not for the love of God, but for the sake of the expansion and luxury of the religious scholars. No one can go to heaven by fighting It is anti-human

11. Can an idol be worshiped as a god?

First of all, it can be said that God is basically a fiction and a belief No one saw him So there is no picture or image of God This is basically the action of fools God is a formless personality If a person worships God by setting up an idol, then it must be wrong So the worship of God will not be with idols

12. Is there anything wrong with the promoter of religion?

Educated people in our country also say that there is nothing wrong with the founders and promoters of any religion sent by God. But a misconception and belief 7 These are the result of excessive faith But every human being is wrong Whether he is a famous person or the founder of religion Because he is not God or instrument He is a man God cannot be wrong, and any instrument that goes wrong will do its intended work. But people can't do that Many say he is human but different What could be wrong with the best man It can never be wrong, the words that come out of his mouth are the truth Those who say these things are very orthodox, that is the result of his teaching This is not true of great human beings, but they also have innumerable mistakes That is why their dignity is diminished, but it is not I will say great people are great There is no doubt that the point But those who say that there is nothing wrong with the initiators of religion, So were they angels? They did not eat, did not urinate, did not do any work They are also human 6 Man is only wrong, that is, man must be wrong, but he is much higher and more dignified than the common man.

13. Do all the dreams of spiritual people come true?

Dream is an erroneous thought and imaginary form Which is not real Fictional image only 6 However, many dreams come true That is a different matter Dreams are basically three types 1 worldly thoughts 2 liberal disturbances 3 fictional I There is also a kind of dream, but the lucky person And the lucky person is not everyone, be it a semi-spiritual person or someone else The dream of a spiritual person is true, but not all dreams There may be a few in a hundred, so this does not mean that his dream does not come true, but not less than all I Those who believe that all the dreams of the spiritual people come true, then maybe they love the spiritual person more. This is the result of his greater love and faith However, judging by the analysis, it is understood that dream means wrong thinking Dreams are not dreams come true More realistic thoughts can be seen in dreams That is, a person who praises or worships God all day long, thinks of Him, But can't that thought come in that dream? And this is how most of the dreams come A spiritual man dreamed that he had intercourse with his wife, but in reality his wife would have children. No, it is never possible This attitude usually comes from uneducated religious pundits A well-educated, wise and pious person can never think of that However, many are educated, yet they speak and understand wrong

14. Is there anything that can be found by worshiping idols or pictures?

If you want something by worshiping an idol or a picture, that is, a picture of God, what do you get? First of all, I would say that there is no image or image of God, so there is no question of asking anything for an image or image of God. Because God is basically fiction and faith is just that No one saw Tina, but she did

15. If you ask God for forgiveness, you will forgive everything

God is basically forgiving God can do everything, there is nothing beyond Him But he does not do that, that is, he does not forgive everyone He basically forgives those who are with God, but not with the person That is, if you blame someone, you have to take forgiveness from him, God has nothing to do there

16. Will heaven be gained only by worshiping God?

Some rural religious people believe that worshiping God alone is not what pleases God. That is the work of God To steal, or to commit adultery, is to worship a god This is what some devotees of God and religion teachers say But is it really the right thing to do? In addition to worshiping God, one has to turn away from the evil ways one by one, then the true God can be a lover. But I don't know when this orthodoxy will go away, but as long as there is religion in my mind, orthodoxy will remain. And basically orthodoxy is born out of most religions

17. Is it true that a follower of one religion and a follower of another religion are looked upon with hatred?

First of all, it is normal to hate followers of one religion and followers of another. Because it is basically the result of illiteracy and orthodoxy of family and environment from childhood There are many religious people who take a bath when they touch the body, name or see some animals but do not have a religious attitude. High religious people do not eat in the homes of many small nations Even reading books in other religious languages shows a religious attitude and makes fun of him But are these really 6? Not right Because these are the highest stages of inhumanity, from which the chances of human return are very low These are basically orthodoxy and anti-religion But these works are usually done by religious people and religion teachers

18. According to many, reading books of other religions is a crime

Even after getting our modern educated society, a lot of orthodoxy and superstition has remained in the minds of the people These are mainly done in rural environment I was reading another scripture one day, and some people saw it After that, from the next day onwards, the highlight is whether I have become irreligious or not Publicity in the neighborhood 7 At that time I was not angry at all, because I know that the work of a farmer is like that of a farmer That is to say, it is proved here how much orthodoxy has taken place in the minds of the people Even educated people did not let me be ridiculed A person can take any language or religious text for education, but those who oppose it, their degree is uneducated orthodoxy.

19. Religion teachers are the right way to earn money to spread the message of religion.

Usually we get education, work, business, and make a living by doing our own work These are basically our daily routine These are our actions That is, education helps us to increase our knowledge and make a living But religion is a different matter and a spiritual matter It is basically the virtue and characteristic of the human race Which will benefit God

Generally, general education is basically all that everyone needs, but religion is all and divine education and necessity This is a good way to go And this divine teaching needs to be given to the religious teachers for free, but they are exploiting it from their religious grandfathers to increase their prestige, sucking and enriching themselves. One class is working in religion and one class is sucking the workers My question here is, why don't you go to school, get educated and get a job, some do business, some do your own work, but as a religious teacher do not get a job, do business, do your own work. They also read later, they work and why they do business in the name of religion Is that right? Is it really a religious principle, Not to pursue one's own interests through religion Which one? A religious guru can never take money for advice Because he is worried about God Many people may ask here, does he not have stomach, what will he eat? Yes, of course Tina has a belly, a wife and a son That is why he cannot do business in the name of religion Because he is a divine devotee The Almighty God sent human beings to fulfill their needs before they were sent to earth Hands, feet, eyes, nose, ears, whatever you need, that is, what you need to do But the way ordinary people are educated and find work or place of work, but why don't they do it? Not all of them are handicapped According to the calculations, God usually needs to be more responsible to human beings than they are, But in that case, why should they get their hands on ordinary working people to feed themselves? At least in that case he could ask God, but why not ask people? Nor do they seek God And if he does not get it from God, then he will work hard and eat like five others Many may say that those who work hard to become religious teachers do not have respect If anyone thinks this, then my question to Tina, maybe it would be nice to beg from ordinary people They can do it the way five people earn, but they can't do it There is a saying, "Who does the exercise when the next one gets it" - written by NK Mandal They have no respect for those who work hard and become religious teachers If anyone thinks this, then my question to Tina, maybe it would be nice to beg from ordinary people They can do it the way five people earn, but they can't do it There is a saying,

"Who does the exercise when the next one gets it" - written by NK Mandal They have no respect for those who work hard and become religious teachers If anyone thinks this, then my question to Tina, maybe it would be nice to beg from ordinary people They can do it the way five people earn, but they can't do it There is a saying, "Who does the exercise when the next one gets it" - written by NK Mandal

I would like to put it bluntly that those who earn their living through religious education are not religious businessmen or religious butchers. It is the work of the clergy to convey God's advice and message to the common people, and that is unconditionally and unselfishly. Let the monotheistic teacher do the work of Tina's family, as the other five do, and give religious instruction in time, then there will be the divine pursuit of religion and religious guru.

20. What is the need of many religious schools in an area?

At first I oppose None of us are basically against education, but we think it is better to leave it when it becomes a business and a foolish society. We are not against religion but for the right religion And that is why it is not right to accept injustice by understanding the face He gave wisdom to man to judge A high school in a large area can accommodate tens of thousands of students, but observation of the area reveals the need for five or seven religious educational institutions. There could have been one And in all those educational institutions there are ten to twenty students If all the educational institutions together could be approved by the government with a big and beautiful general education But they do not do that In addition to religious lessons, the name only gives general education, but also training by uneducated teachers They do this mainly for their own benefit, Because you have to eat something one by one They will not be able to get a job and will not be able to work, so there is only one way, business in the name of religion. If five of the seven religious educational institutions were not one in one area, then religious education could be improved. And in all those educational institutions, students will not be human, nor will Munish Maybe a beggar or a businessman in the name of the only religion And the cost of all those educational institutions comes from the common man In this the common man lacks money and religion goes to the merchants An area can run a high school with ten villages, but why can't a religious school run, when a high school has a few students from each village. But in the school of religion, each village may be one or two Then how many religious institutions are needed in an area? As a result, there is only one way, business in the name of religion If five of the seven religious educational institutions were not one in one area, then religious education could be improved. And in all those educational institutions, students will not be human, nor will Munish Maybe a beggar or a businessman in the name of the only religion And the cost of all those educational institutions comes from the common man In this the common man lacks money and religion goes to the merchants An area can run a high school with ten villages, but why can't a religious school run, when a high school has a few students from each village. But in the school of religion, each village may be one or two Then how many religious institutions are needed in an area? As a result, there is only one way, business in the name of religion If five of the seven religious educational institutions were not one in one area, then religious education could be improved. And in all those educational institutions, students will not be human, nor will Munish Maybe a beggar or a businessman in the name of the only religion And the cost of all those educational institutions comes from the common man In this the common man lacks money and religion goes to the merchants An area can run a high school with ten villages, but why can't a religious school run, when a high school has a few students from each village. But in the school of religion, each village may be one or two Then how many religious institutions are needed in an area? However, religious education could have been improved And in all those educational institutions, students will not be human, nor will Munish Maybe a beggar or a businessman in the name of the only religion And the cost of all those educational institutions comes from the common man In this the common man lacks money and religion goes to the merchants An area can run a high school with ten villages, but why can't a religious school run, when a high school has a few students from each village. But in the school of religion, each village may be one or two Then how many religious institutions are needed in an area? However, religious education could have been improved And in all those educational institutions, students will not be human, nor will Munish Maybe a beggar or a businessman in the name of the only religion And the cost of all those educational institutions comes from the common man In this the common man lacks money and religion goes to the merchants An area can run a high school with ten villages, but why can't a religious school run, when a high school has a few students from each village. But in the school of religion, each village may be one or two Then how many religious institutions are needed in an area? Munish 6 will not Maybe a beggar or a businessman in the name of the only religion And the cost of all those educational institutions comes from the common man In this the common man lacks money and religion goes to the merchants An area can run a high school with ten villages, but why can't a religious school run, when a high school has a few students from each village. But in the school of religion, each village may be one or two Then how many religious institutions are needed in an area? Munish 6 will not Maybe a beggar or a businessman in the name of the only religion And the cost of all those educational institutions comes from the common man In this the common man lacks money and religion goes to the merchants An area can run a high school with ten villages, but why can't a religious school run, when a high school has a few students from each village. But in the school of religion, each village may be one or two Then how many religious institutions are needed in an area?

21. Is state religion important in the state?

State religion is the religion approved by the state government It is basically a secret religion according to the majority of the religious population But in fact, state religion is not beneficial at all Rather, it is for a dangerous state In a country where the state religion is enshrined in the constitution, minorities are in danger at every turn. The majority of the people became religious extremists Whatever his religion is The country cannot run with religious law in any country, but the progress of the country will go back hundreds of years If that were the case, then one of the one hundred and ninety-five countries in the world today would not have a complete set of religious laws, even if they were just a few drops. The state benefits a class of politicians by religion, but not a drop of religion. On the contrary, extremism, bigotry, militancy, and terror are rampant in the country, which is enough to destroy the country's progress and society. Not only that, there is a lot of violence, brutality, oppression,

I think the state religion is a danger to the country, why not a free thinker who has the privilege of speaking but can't speak out against the religious gurus and disciples, meaning there is no freedom of speech even though the religion gurus say whatever they want, They do not have difficulty In a religious state, the people do not have freedom of speech, they oppose what they eat, where they go, what they wear, who they do, and they are severely punished by a religious organization called Samaj.

Second, religion is a non-governmental organization But the state is a government organization The law that the state will make applies to everyone, but the law is prescribed for religious followers, but not for other non-religious people, but when non-religious people speak against religious law, it becomes a conflict. Of course, it is natural to throw stones at someone, but it is a matter of action. That is, both religion and unrighteousness are opposite The work of the two is different When religion does not speak against unrighteousness, the pious will not understand anything Similarly, if free thinkers do not speak against religion, then free thinkers will not understand anything. But this free thinker is threatened whenever he goes to say something, but nothing happens when religion speaks against the free thinker.

| | Chapter III | |

Orthodoxy

1. Is Pharaoh the only preserving corpse in Egypt?

Some of our Bengali grandfathers believed that Pharaoh was the only preserved corpse on earth and in Egypt, and that it was a sign of God. So that the people of the world may understand that God has really done this to show man Many think that Pharaoh is the wrath of God

Pharaoh is not the name of a person, it is a misconception Pharaoh or Pharaoh is the title of the central ruler of Egypt Such as Raja, Nawab Badshah, Sultan etc. 7 There is, however, a difference of opinion as to the name of the Pharaoh, whom the pious fathers have exaggerated. Someone said, Qaboos, Ramesses and Ramesses II But according to various sources, his real name was Ramesses II, and his father's name was Siba.

Some Bengalis believe that Pharaoh's body was under water for hundreds of years And they all believe that Pharaoh did this because he opposed the preacher of God. The fruit of sin 6 থাকনেThati ঈTyadi says But in fact these are misconceptions of human beings And completely rumors and lies

First of all, the body of a dead person cannot exist for a hundred years And was there no one more sinful than Pharaoh? The dead human body is perishable, its religion is perishable, it is perishable Usually the dead body cannot stay in water for more than five to seven days

Second, the dead body is usually floating, not under water In other words, the researcher has lied for the sake of someone

For this reason, researchers have shown evidence of salt 7 found evidence of salt in Pharaoh's body Of course it is normal It is true that you have found evidence of salt But this is not to say that salt was found in Pharaoh's body to stay under water

Thirdly, there is no evidence that Pharaoh's body was recovered That is, who rescued from the bottom of the water, when did 7 How many floors were there? কেউNo one knows the subject yet I All that is known is that there is a pharaoh's body in a museum in Egypt, and many researchers have researched it, but no one has been able to give accurate information that Pharaoh was actually under water. Only Dr. Maurice Bucaille said that Pharaoh was under water, and Dr. Maurice Bucaille thinks salt was found in the body to stay underwater. But the head said. Maurice Bucaille does not know that Egyptians are famous for mummies and pyramids and that Egypt is called the land of mummies and pyramids. In other words, to make a mummy, you need salt, glue, paint, cloth, wood, etc. Therefore, it is easy to say that the salt found in the body of the corpse only took time to make the mummy. There are also many mummies older than the mummy of Pharaoh Ramesses II

Dr. fourth. Maurice Bucaille is an Arab health doctor, not a scientist or a body researcher. Bucaille was a physician, not a scientist, originally from the Saudi royal family A health doctor cannot examine a dead body because he has not studied it The work of corpse research is not the work of a skilled scientist but of a physician As knowledge and wisdom are not one That is, after acquiring knowledge first, it becomes wise if it is skill That is Dr. Maurice Bucaille did not study as a researcher In other words, the Saudi government has fabricated a lie with an established doctor And I think this is the belief of some Bengalis

2. Are idols and sculptures the same type?

Statues or sculptures are not one Two separate things 6 Many people confuse them I think it's one thing, but it's not Idol lexical meaning is idol 8 It is, of course, the female gender language Idol, of course, refers to both men and women Idols are basically objects of worship or venerable But it is considered anti-religion As I myself am against idol worship But I am not against sculpture Sculpture is basically an object of respect Sculpture is not an object of worship or veneration It is an object of tradition and honor Many people argue that these two are one, but they do not know it, because it is not practiced in the practice of knowledge.

But idols can be objects of worship but not an indicator of tradition and honor It can be a sign of honor in terms of worship or object of worship, but it cannot be just a sign of respect by a particular group, it has to be universal. But sculpture as a whole is an indicator of honor Like any proud person in our country Example - Dr. APJ Abdul Kalam Sir 6

3. What exactly is self-reflection?

In our Indian subcontinent, it is customary to take one's own image or picture, drawing is anti-God and anti-scripture. Many people think so, because they say that if you can make a picture or painting, you can establish life Of course, it is true that life cannot be established in pictures or paintings, but it is not that pictures or paintings cannot be established. Those who say that it is not true are in fact believers in orthodoxy and erroneous beliefs সৃত All individuals further delay the progress of the country and society

If we speak according to them, then it is seen that they are liars and businessmen

First of all, they say that nothing happens without God And all the knowledge of man is given by God He wants the welfare of all He never wants evil That is to say, the knowledge given to the scientist belongs to that God If he disliked taking pictures or painting, he would not give knowledge to that scientific head And if he didn't give knowledge to the scientist's head, the scientist would never be able to make pictures or paintings So did God want pictures or paintings?

And if there was no God or what these people wanted, what could they do? In fact, God wants the society, country and nation to be developed But there are some people who oppose them But in fact, some businessmen are trying to suppress the society, country and progress.